FINDING
your inner
KINK

(A kink journal to help you discover
your inner fantasies and kinks)

This Journal belongs to
to

_____

What made you decide it was time to find out what your inner kink is and what you really want sexually?

_____

_____

_____

_____

_____

_____

_____

_____

_____

_____

_____

_____

_____

_____

"

Don't Worry...

It only seems kinky the first time

Some Common Kinks...

Which of these kinks appeal to you the most?

1. BDSM

BDSM is all about one party exerting dominance over the other in a mutually consensual, pre-agreed-upon, and satisfying encounter. This kink is for you if you fantasize about letting your partner have their way with you, or if you derive pleasure from the idea of "making" your partner service and please you.

2. Sadism and Masochism

These kinks are all about your relationship to pain. A sadist derives pleasure from inflicting pain on a sexual partner, and a masochist derives pleasure from receiving it.

3. Hosiery

This kink is marked by an interest in wearing pantyhose or having a partner wear hosiery while engaging in sexual activity. If you find that you often ask your partner to wear hosiery, or you yourself feel a strong urge to wear them during sex and experience more pleasure when wearing or seeing hosiery, you may have a pantyhose fetish or kink.

4. Exhibitionism

This kink is all about getting turned on by being observed. If you ever fantasize about having sex, masturbating, or getting naked in front of an audience or want someone to watch you, then you might find this kink enjoyable.

Some Common Kinks...

Which of these kinks appeal to you the most?

5. Voyeurism

A voyeurism kink centers on being turned on by watching other people having sex. You might figure out that this is your kink by being particularly turned on by seeing yourself have sex in a mirror.

6. Dirtytalk

This might be your kink if you're generally verbose and enjoy using words to feel powerful during sex. You'll know if this is your kink or not if you reach orgasm quicker when talking or being talked to.

7. Roleplay

This kink is defined by taking on different personas during sex and experiencing intensified pleasure from stepping outside of yourself. Are you usually shy but really let go and come harder when you don't have to be yourself? Maybe roleplay is your kink.

8. Nipple play

People who in general find themselves drawn to breasts might find they have a nipple kink. Tweak, lick, and bite your partner's nipples or invite them to do so to yours in order to discover if this is the kink for you. Plus, nipple play isn't just for women, men also enjoy their nipples played with

Some Common Kinks...

Which of these kinks appeal to you the most?

9. Urophilia

Also known as piss play, golden showers, or watersports, this kink is for folks who are sexually aroused by urination, either giving or receiving. You can ease into piss play by starting in the shower and seeing how it feels. This kink may be more likely to appeal to you if you're also interested in domination or submission.

10. Cuckolding

This kink tends to be more common among men but can be appealing to all genders as well. Cuckolding is about being turned on by your partner having sex with someone else, either in front of you or away from you, and relaying details at a later date. A cuckold is aroused by the idea of sharing their partner and also by the implied humiliation of "not being able to wholly satisfy" them.

11. Female-led Relationships

People with an FLR kink are turned on by giving the woman in a heterosexual relationship the bulk of the sexual control. This could look like sex centering on her pleasure or her deciding when and how sex should be had.

12. Financial Domination

AKA FinDom is often a fetish but can also be a kink. It involves giving over total control of one's finances to someone else or being kept on a strict budget or being ordered to purchase certain things.

Some Common Kinks...
Which of these kinks appeal to you the most?

13. Auralism

Also known as having a sound kink, i.e. being turned on by hearing things. For example, you might be extra aroused by hearing the sound of your partner hitting against you as you have sex or the sound of their moans or how wet they are. You can explore this kink by trying to dampen out other senses, by using a blindfold for instance, so you can focus on the noises. If you've ever gotten tingly listening to ASMR or the sound effects in audio erotica, this might be your kink.

14. Orgasm Control

This kink is common among people who are generally interested in BDSM. It's exactly what it says on the tin: letting your partner control the timing of your orgasm. This is often achieved through the use of bondage.

15. Gags

Having a gag kink can mean that you're turned on by wearing or making your partner wear a gag of some kind. It's important when exploring this kink that the person who is gagged can still communicate.

16. Praise Kink

Someone with a praise kink is aroused by compliments, praise, and encouragement, for instance, being told 'You're doing such a good job, taking my cock, or You're so beautiful when you...' While most people like to receive compliments, someone with a praise kink will be really sent over the edge by receiving them in a sexual setting.

YES, NO, MAYBE??

What do you want to try? Is it a yes, a no, or a maybe? Have some fun as you go through the list.

	YES	NO	MAYBE
Anywhere but the bed sex			
Have a threesome			
Engage in group sex (orgy)			
Have sex with the same gender			
Be a voyeur and watch others have sex			
Have sex with someone old enough to be your dad/mom			
Sex with an escort			
Finger yourself in front of someone while they watch			
Film yourself having sex (keep the tape safe!!!)			
Give your man a blowjob while he is driving			
Have sex in an elevator			
Use ice in your mouth while giving oral sex			
Mutually masturbate each other			

YES, NO, MAYBE??

What do you want to try? Is it a yes, a no, or a maybe? Have some fun as you go through the list.

	YES	NO	MAYBE
Have sex wearing restraints			
Have a hot makeout session in a busy place			
Play strip poker			
Have sex in your workplace			
Have a moresome (sex with more than 3 people)			
Sex in a haunted house			
Footjob			
Pegging aka strap-on			
Anilingus (anal sex)			
Consensual non consent (rape roleplay)			
Use a leash and a collar to have sex			
Sex in a graveyard			
Have sex on a nude beach			

YES, NO, MAYBE??

What do you want to try? Is it a yes, a no, or a maybe? Have some fun as you go through the list.

	YES	NO	MAYBE
Have loud as fuck sex			
Masturbate with your partner together and finish			
Sex in a different positions not repeating the same one			
Have sex by a window			
Have a quickie in a public place			
Try Role playing			
Cook naked in front of your partner			
Try a remote controlled sex toy and let your partner play with it			
Foreplay sex. No penetration			
Skinny dipping			
Read erotica to your partner or do it together			
Sex on a washing machine			
Get frisky at a wedding			

KINK Bucket List

Create your own sexy bucket list

○ _____

○ _____

○ _____

○ _____

○ _____

○ _____

○ _____

○ _____

○ _____

○ _____

○ _____

○ _____

○ _____

○ _____

○ _____

○ _____

○ _____

○ _____

KINK Bucket List

Create your own sexy bucket list

- ⭘ _____
- ⭘ _____
- ⭘ _____
- ⭘ _____
- ⭘ _____
- ⭘ _____
- ⭘ _____
- ⭘ _____
- ⭘ _____
- ⭘ _____
- ⭘ _____
- ⭘ _____
- ⭘ _____
- ⭘ _____
- ⭘ _____
- ⭘ _____
- ⭘ _____
- ⭘ _____

KINK Bucket List
Create your own sexy bucket list

○ _____

○ _____

○ _____

○ _____

○ _____

○ _____

○ _____

○ _____

○ _____

○ _____

○ _____

○ _____

○ _____

○ _____

○ _____

○ _____

○ _____

○ _____

Kinky Challenges
Do you have the balls to do it???

Have sex while wearing blindfolds. Both of you
Did you do it? How did it go?

Have a hot makeout session without touching each other.
Did you do it? How did it go?

Kinky Challenges
Do you have the balls to do it???

See how many times you can have sex in one day
without reusing any of the same positions
Did you do it? How did it go?

Mimic a porn scene
Did you do it? How did it go?

Kinky Challenges
Do you have the balls to do it???

Have sex fully clothed

Did you do it? How did it go?

Have sex with the most unsexy playlist

Did you do it? How did it go?

Kinky Challenges
Do you have the balls to do it???

Create and formulate a new sex position
Did you do it? How did it go?

Use all your sex toys during your sex session
Did you do it? How did it go?

Kinky Challenges
Do you have the balls to do it???

Buy a new sex toy you have never used and use it.
Did you do it? How did it go?

Have silent sex. No moans or grunts.
Did you do it? How did it go?

Kinky Challenges
Do you have the balls to do it???

Have sex without kissing your partner.
Did you do it? How did it go?

Dirty talk in a foreign language.
Did you do it? How did it go?

Kinky Challenges
Do you have the balls to do it???

Buy a book of sex positions and recreate what you
see when you open the book randomly

Did you do it? How did it go?

Have sex while standing. Don't lean on anything.
Did you do it? How did it go?

If I am going to be a mess, I
might as well be a hot mess

Right?

UNLEASH your inner

KINK

Your Innner Kink

What does being submissive mean to you?

_____

_____

_____

_____

_____

_____

_____

_____

_____

_____

_____

_____

_____

_____

Your Innner Kink

Describe the actions, traits, and thought that best describe submission to you.

_____

_____

_____

_____

_____

_____

_____

_____

_____

_____

_____

_____

_____

_____

_____

Your Innner Kink

What counts as kinks to you?

_____

_____

_____

_____

_____

_____

_____

_____

_____

_____

_____

_____

_____

_____

Your Innner Kink

Describe your best kinky self.

_____

_____

_____

_____

_____

_____

_____

_____

_____

_____

_____

_____

_____

_____

Your Innner Kink

List 10 things about your kinky self.

_____

_____

_____

_____

_____

_____

_____

_____

_____

_____

_____

_____

_____

_____

Your Innner Kink

Make a list of your kinks.

_____

_____

_____

_____

_____

_____

_____

_____

_____

_____

_____

_____

_____

_____

Your Innner Kink

When you were younger, what kind of fantasies excited you?

_____

_____

_____

_____

_____

_____

_____

_____

_____

_____

_____

_____

_____

_____

Your Innner Kink

Did you understand what these fantasies in your childhood meant?

_____

_____

_____

_____

_____

_____

_____

_____

_____

_____

_____

_____

_____

_____

Your Innner Kink

Did you try to act your fantasies out? What was your experience?

_____

_____

_____

_____

_____

_____

_____

_____

_____

_____

_____

_____

_____

Your Innner Kink

What counts as sex to you?

_____

_____

_____

_____

_____

_____

_____

_____

_____

_____

_____

_____

_____

_____

Your Innner Kink

What was your first sexual experience like?

_____

_____

_____

_____

_____

_____

_____

_____

_____

_____

_____

_____

_____

_____

Your Innner Kink

List 3 turn-ons during kinky play.

_____

_____

_____

_____

_____

_____

_____

_____

_____

_____

_____

_____

_____

_____

Your Innner Kink

List 3 turn-offs during kinky play.

_____

_____

_____

_____

_____

_____

_____

_____

_____

_____

_____

_____

Your Innner Kink

Did you have any early signs, concerning your kinks?

_____

_____

_____

_____

_____

_____

_____

_____

_____

_____

_____

_____

_____

_____

_____

Your Innner Kink

Did you ever feel shame because of your fantasies?

_____

_____

_____

_____

_____

_____

_____

_____

_____

_____

_____

_____

_____

Your Innner Kink

What did you do to become more in touch with yourself and your kinks?

_____

_____

_____

_____

_____

_____

_____

_____

_____

_____

_____

_____

_____

Your Innner Kink

Describe your weirdest sexual fantasy.

_____

_____

_____

_____

_____

_____

_____

_____

_____

_____

_____

_____

_____

_____

Your Innner Kink

Describe your most exciting sexual fantasy.

_____

_____

_____

_____

_____

_____

_____

_____

_____

_____

_____

_____

_____

_____

Your Innner Kink

What is your favorite toy?

_____

_____

_____

_____

_____

_____

_____

_____

_____

_____

_____

_____

_____

_____

_____

_____

Your Innner Kink

Do you read books about BDSM? What is your favorite?

_____

_____

_____

_____

_____

_____

_____

_____

_____

_____

_____

_____

_____

_____

Your Innner Kink

Write down, on a piece of paper a BDSM or kink act you would like to try?

_____

_____

_____

_____

_____

_____

_____

_____

_____

_____

_____

_____

Your Innner Kink

Are there any acts in the movie that you would want to try?

_____

_____

_____

_____

_____

_____

_____

_____

_____

_____

_____

_____

_____

Your Innner Kink

Does your non-kinky interest sometimes find its way into your kinky activities? If so, how?

_____

_____

_____

_____

_____

_____

_____

_____

_____

_____

_____

_____

_____

Your Innner Kink

Make a detailed explanation of your wants and needs.

_____

_____

_____

_____

_____

_____

_____

_____

_____

_____

_____

_____

_____

_____

Your Innner Kink

Make a detailed explanation of your fears and fetishes.

_____

_____

_____

_____

_____

_____

_____

_____

_____

_____

_____

_____

_____

_____

Your Innner Kink

Make a list of what turns you on.

_____

_____

_____

_____

_____

_____

_____

_____

_____

_____

_____

_____

_____

_____

Your Innner Kink

What is one thing you want to be done to you, but feel ashamed to state?

_____

_____

_____

_____

_____

_____

_____

_____

_____

_____

_____

_____

_____

Your Innner Kink

What normal things in life do you now see differently
because of your kinks and fetish?

_____

_____

_____

_____

_____

_____

_____

_____

_____

_____

_____

_____

_____

Your Innner Kink

Do you think you would be happy in a vanilla relationship?
Why or why not?

_____

_____

_____

_____

_____

_____

_____

_____

_____

_____

_____

_____

Your Innner Kink

What is something that may stop you from pursuing a vanilla relationship?

_____

_____

_____

_____

_____

_____

_____

_____

_____

_____

_____

_____

_____

Your Innner Kink

Have you had any recent mindset change or shift regarding your kinks and fetishes?

_____

_____

_____

_____

_____

_____

_____

_____

_____

_____

_____

_____

_____

_____

Your Innner Kink

How have these mindset shifts affected you?

_____

_____

_____

_____

_____

_____

_____

_____

_____

_____

_____

_____

_____

_____

Your Innner Kink

How long did it take you to accept your sexual fetishes and kinks?

_____

_____

_____

_____

_____

_____

_____

_____

_____

_____

_____

_____

Your Innner Kink

Why did you take that long to do so?

_____

_____

_____

_____

_____

_____

_____

_____

_____

_____

_____

_____

_____

_____

Your Innner Kink

What hindrances did you face in the process of accepting who you are?

_____

_____

_____

_____

_____

_____

_____

_____

_____

_____

_____

_____

_____

Your Innner Kink

Write out your preferred kinks and fetishes and give them a rating between 1-5.

_____

_____

_____

_____

_____

_____

_____

_____

_____

_____

_____

_____

_____

Your Innner Kink

Have you ever tried to play solo? How did that turn out?

_____

_____

_____

_____

_____

_____

_____

_____

_____

_____

_____

_____

_____

Your Innner Kink

Rate your communication on a scale of 1-10

_____

_____

_____

_____

_____

_____

_____

_____

_____

_____

_____

_____

_____

_____

_____

Your Innner Kink

What do you look back on, over the past year and learn?

_____

_____

_____

_____

_____

_____

_____

_____

_____

_____

_____

_____

_____

_____

Your Innner Kink

What do you look back on, over the past year and loved?

_____

_____

_____

_____

_____

_____

_____

_____

_____

_____

_____

_____

_____

_____

Your Innner Kink

What are some things you had to change in yourself this past year?

_____

_____

_____

_____

_____

_____

_____

_____

_____

_____

_____

_____

_____

Your Innner Kink

What are 5 myths about BDSM that you have heard?

_____

_____

_____

_____

_____

_____

_____

_____

_____

_____

_____

_____

_____

_____

Your Innner Kink

What are the truths to these myths?

_____

_____

_____

_____

_____

_____

_____

_____

_____

_____

_____

_____

_____

Your Innner Kink

Have you ever been fascinated lately by people in vanilla relationships?

_____

_____

_____

_____

_____

_____

_____

_____

_____

_____

_____

_____

_____

_____

Your Innner Kink

What are some things they do that no longer entice you?

_____

_____

_____

_____

_____

_____

_____

_____

_____

_____

_____

_____

_____

Your Innner Kink

What was your first introduction to BDSM?

_____

_____

_____

_____

_____

_____

_____

_____

_____

_____

_____

_____

_____

_____

Your Innner Kink

What parts/areas of BDSM excites you?

_____

_____

_____

_____

_____

_____

_____

_____

_____

_____

_____

_____

_____

Your Innner Kink

In your words, what does it mean for a person to submit to another in the context of the BDSM lifestyle?

_____

_____

_____

_____

_____

_____

_____

_____

_____

_____

_____

_____

_____

_____

Your Innner Kink

Write out what you want in BDSM play.

_____

_____

_____

_____

_____

_____

_____

_____

_____

_____

_____

_____

_____

_____

Your Innner Kink

What feelings engulf you when you think about being submissive?

_____

_____

_____

_____

_____

_____

_____

_____

_____

_____

_____

_____

_____

Your Innner Kink

What is the difference between a submissive, a bottom, a baby girl, and a slave?

_____

_____

_____

_____

_____

_____

_____

_____

_____

_____

_____

_____

Your Innner Kink

What is the difference between a dominant, a top, a master, and a daddy?

_____

_____

_____

_____

_____

_____

_____

_____

_____

_____

_____

_____

_____

Your Innner Kink

What is the most difficult part of having a sexuality that involves BDSM?

_____

_____

_____

_____

_____

_____

_____

_____

_____

_____

_____

_____

_____

_____

Your Innner Kink

Describe your dream BDSM act and how you want it to play out.

_____

_____

_____

_____

_____

_____

_____

_____

_____

_____

_____

_____

_____

Your Innner Kink

What are some of the things you will and will not do?

_____

_____

_____

_____

_____

_____

_____

_____

_____

_____

_____

_____

_____

_____

_____

_____

"

Confidence is when you have
the power and ability to do what
you want, and say what you
want with no shame

NOTES

NOTES

NOTES

NOTES

NOTES

NOTES

NOTES

NOTES

NOTES

NOTES

NOTES

Made in the USA
Columbia, SC
28 October 2024